Apes and Monkeys

KINGFISHER

Kingfisher Publications Plc
New Penderel House
283–288 High Holborn
London WC1V 7HZ
www.kingfisherpub.com

First published by Kingfisher Publications Plc 2004
2 4 6 8 10 9 7 5 3 1
ZIP-TS/0806/PROSP/RNB(RNB)/140MA/F

A CIP catalogue record for this book is available from the British Library.

ISBN: 978 0 7534 1052 3

Senior editor: Belinda Weber
Senior designer: Carol Ann Davis
Cover designer: Anthony Cutting
Picture manager: Cee Weston-Baker
Picture researcher: Harriet Merry
DTP manager: Nicky Studdart
Artwork archivists: Wendy Allison, Jenny Lord
Production manager: Nancy Roberts
Indexer: Chris Bernstein

Printed in China

Acknowledgements
The publishers would like to thank the following for permission to reproduce their material. Every care has been taken
to trace copyright holders. However, if there have been unintentional omissions or failure to trace copyright holders,
we apologise and will, if informed, endeavour to make corrections in any future edition.
b = bottom, c = centre, l = left, t = top, r = right

Photographs: *cover* Getty; 4–5 Steve Bloom; 6–7 Oxford Scientific Films; 8 Martin Harvey/NHPA; 9 Ardea; 10–11 Ardea; 11*tl* Oxford
Scientific Films; 12*br* Oxford Scientific Films; 13*tl* Oxford Scientific Films; 14 Ardea; 15*t* Rojer Eritja/Alamy; 15*b* Steve Bloom; 16 Oxford
Scientific Films; 17 Steve Bloom; 18*b* Anup Shah/Nature Picture Library; 20*tr* Oxford Scientific Film; 22*b* Steve Bloom; 23*tr* Peter
Blackwell/Nature Picture Library; 23*l* Art Wolfe/Getty Images; 23*br* James Warwick/NHPA; 24*bl* Ardea; 24–25 Steve Bloom; 25*br* Ardea;
26*bl* Kevin Schafer/Corbis; 26*t* Tony Hamblin/Corbis; 29 Mark Bowler/NHPA; 30–31*b* Richard du Toit/NHPA; 31*tl* Anup Shah/Nature Picture
Library; 31 Roland Seitre/Still Pictures; 32*bl* Oxford Scientific Films; 32*br* Ardea; 33*tl* Oxford Scientific Films; 33*r* Anup Shah/Nature Picture
Library; 34*bl* Theo Allofs/Corbis; 34*r* Ardea; 35 Steve Bloom; 36*b* Anup Shah/Nature Picture Library; 36*t* Getty Images; 37*tl* Dietmar
Nill/Nature Picture Library; 37*b* Frank Lane Picture Agency; 38*b* Anup Shah/Nature Picture Library; 38*t* Ardea; 39 Getty Images; 40*tl* Ardea;
40*b* Karl Ammann/Nature Picture Library; 41 Ardea; 48 Steve Bloom

Commissioned photography on pages 42–47 by Andy Crawford. Project-maker and photoshoot co-ordinator: Miranda Kennedy
Thank you to models Aaron Hibbert, Lewis Manu, Alastair Roper and Rebecca Roper

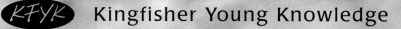

Kingfisher Young Knowledge

Apes and Monkeys

Barbara Taylor

Contents

What is an ape?

You are one! There are four other great apes – gorillas, chimpanzees (chimps), orang-utans and bonobos. Gibbons are small apes. Apes have gripping fingers and thumbs and no tail.

Hairy apes

Apes are a kind of mammal, which is an animal with a hairy body. Hair helps to keep mammals warm. We have much less hair than the other apes, such as this gorilla.

mammal – *a hairy animal that feeds its babies on mother's milk*

Brainy apes

All apes have a big brain and are clever. They can solve problems, use tools, remember things and communicate with each other. Humans are the only apes that speak.

Arms and legs

Most apes' arms are longer than their legs. They can swing through the trees or walk on all fours. Humans walk upright on long legs.

communicate – *make other animals understand your message*

Apes in Africa

Three big wild apes live in the forests, woodlands and mountains of Africa. These are gorillas, bonobos and chimps. They all live in large groups.

Gorilla groups

Gorillas live in peaceful groups with between five and 20 members. The group of males, females and young is led by a big male.

bonobo

chimpanzee

Girl power

Bonobos look like chimps but are more graceful. They have smaller heads and ears and longer legs than chimps. Female bonobos lead the groups.

Noisy chimpanzees

Chimps live in the biggest groups, with up to 100 members. A few important male chimps lead each group. Chimps are noisier and fight more often than the other African apes.

forests – *places with lots of trees*

Apes in Asia

Orang-utans and gibbons are apes that live in Asia. They spend a lot of time in trees, although male orang-utans have to climb down sometimes, as they grow too big for the branches.

Fatty faces

Male orang-utans have fatty pads the size of dinner plates on their faces. These make them look bigger and help them to scare away any rivals.

rivals – *competitors for food or mates*

Singing apes

Siamang gibbons are the biggest gibbons. They sing to tell other gibbons where they live. Pouches on their throats inflate as they sing, making their voices even louder.

inflate – fill up with air

Getting around

Chimpanzees and gorillas spend a lot of time on the ground. Orang-utans, gibbons and bonobos climb in the trees. Gibbons live high in the tree-tops.

Knuckle walking

When they walk on all fours, chimps rest their weight on thick pads of skin on their knuckles.

Swinging ape

Gibbons swing from branch to branch using first one hand, then the other. They can move very quickly without making much noise.

Hanging on

Orang-utans grip branches tightly with their long, hooked fingers. Their arms can stretch a long way. Each arm is nearly twice as long as each leg!

knuckles – *places where the fingers bend*

Finding food

Apes feed mainly on fruit and leaves but they also eat a small amount of meat, such as insects. Chimps sometimes eat larger animals, including monkeys.

Going fishing!

Chimps chew sticks or grass stems to make them the right shape to dig for food. They push the sticks into a termite mound. When they pull them out, termites are clinging to the end.

Fruit feast

Durian is one of the orang-utan's favourite foods. They remember where to find trees with ripe fruit.

Tasty termites

Millions of termites live inside a termite mound. They can provide a tasty snack for hungry chimpanzees.

Brainy apes

Apes are one of the few animals to make and use tools, which is one sign of an intelligent animal.

Tough nuts to crack

Some chimps bang a heavy stone on to nuts. This works like a hammer and cracks open their hard shells.

Rainy days

Apes do not like the rain because their fur is not very waterproof. This orang-utan has made its own umbrella out of bark.

tools – *objects that help with work*

Chatty chimps

The chimpanzees in a group make different sounds, pull faces and use the position of their bodies to 'talk' to their family and friends.

Pulling faces

With their big eyes and bendy lips, chimps are good at pulling faces. Their expressions show how they are feeling.

Playtime

As young chimps play, they learn how to mix with other chimps in their group. They learn which chimps are the most important in the group.

Sound signals

Chimps use their big ears to listen for sounds drifting through the forest. The members of a group hoot to each other to stay in touch.

Forever friends

Chimps may have special friends in their group. These friends hug each other for comfort and to show that they are still friends.

expression – the 'look' on a face

Baby apes

Apes usually have one baby at a time. They spend many years teaching the baby how to move, feed and behave.

Gibbon families

Gibbons live in small family groups. A gibbon father plays with his baby and helps to look after it.

Riding piggy-back

Many baby apes, such as this gorilla, are carried around until they are strong enough to walk by themselves.

Motherly love

A baby orang-utan lives with its mother for seven to nine years. It does not usually have any other playmates.

What is a monkey?

A monkey is a clever, playful mammal with a tail. It usually lives in groups for safety. There are 130 different monkeys, from tiny tamarins to big baboons.

Living quarters

Monkeys live in a wide range of habitats, from forests and mountains, to grasslands and swamps. These proboscis monkeys live in a swamp.

Terrific tails

Monkey tails can be long or short, thick or thin, straight or curly. This colobus uses its fluffy tail to steer as it leaps through the trees.

Day and night

The owl monkey is the only monkey that comes out at night. It has big eyes to help it see in the dark.

How clever?

Capuchins are intelligent monkeys with a large brain. This helps them to live in a range of different habitats.

habitats – areas where animals live

American monkeys

American monkeys live in the warm rainforests of Central and South America. They have wide, round nostrils that are far apart. Many have prehensile tails that grip like an extra hand.

Finger food

Tamarins have long fingers, which they use to search for their insect food. They have claws instead of fingernails.

Tree-top leapers

Little squirrel monkeys leap through the trees like squirrels, and climb on to thin branches. They live in big groups of up to 200 monkeys.

Furry monkeys

Saki monkeys have long shaggy fur, which helps to protect them from heavy rain. They may suck water off their fur.

prehensile tails – *tails that grip tightly*

African and Asian monkeys

These monkeys have nostrils that are close together, and hard pads on their bottoms to help them sleep sitting up. They do not have prehensile tails.

Packed lunch

The red-tailed monkey stores its food in cheek pouches, then finds a safe place to sit and eat.

Follow the leader

Slim, graceful mona monkeys live in troops of up to 20 monkeys. Each troop is led by a strong male. Monas have striking marks and colours on their soft, thick fur.

Hot baths

Japanese macaques live in the mountains. In the cold, snowy winter, they grow thick coats and sit in hot spring water to keep warm.

troop – a group of monkeys

Spot the difference

Monkeys are smaller than apes and not as clever. Monkeys usually have a tail, but apes never have a tail.

Big ape

Gorillas are the biggest of the wild apes. Female gorillas weigh about half as much as males. The size of the males scares predators and rivals.

predators – animals that hunt and eat other animals

Monkey tails

The spider monkey curls its prehensile tail around branches. The bare, ridged skin under the tail helps it to cling tightly.

Moving and grooving

Monkeys scamper along the tops of branches or run fast along the ground. They do not usually swing through the branches, like the apes.

Feet made for walking

Baboons live on the ground and walk on all fours. They press their fingers on the ground, but keep their palms raised. This lifts their heads, so they can watch for danger. They even walk through water.

Leggy leapers

The long back legs of colobus monkeys help them to push off strongly from branches. They can make huge leaps from tree to tree.

Hanging around

Uakaris live at the tops of tall trees in swampy and flooded forests. They sometimes use their powerful back legs to hang upside-down.

Hungry monkeys

A monkey's favourite food is usually fruit. Monkeys also feed on leaves, nuts, flowers and insects. Some have special diets, such as the marmosets that eat tree gum.

Nuts and seeds

Sakis spend a lot of time eating seeds. Some sakis have strong jaws to crack open hard nuts and reach the soft food stored inside.

Clever capuchin

This capuchin is chewing bark from a small branch. It can also crack open nuts or shells by hitting them on rocks.

Meat for dinner
Baboons are strong, smart and agile enough to catch other monkeys, birds and small antelope.

Green salad
Colobus monkeys mainly eat leaves, but also enjoy munching ripe fruit, flowers and seeds. In their big stomachs, bacteria release energy from their food.

bacteria — *tiny, one-celled lifeforms*

Getting to know you

Monkeys have many ways of keeping in touch. They also use calls, colours and behaviour to find a mate and warn of danger.

Keep away!

Howlers are the world's noisiest land animals! Their calls warn other howlers to keep away.

Bad hair day?

Monkeys and apes groom each other's fur. They pick out any dirt or bugs they find and clean up any scratches. Grooming helps monkeys keep clean and stay friends.

Colour signals

The colours of the male mandrill become brighter when he is healthy, angry or excited. Females prefer males with bright colours.

groom – *pick through fur with fingers*

Baby monkeys

Monkey mothers look after their babies until they are about 12 to 18 months old – a shorter time than apes.

New babies
Baby monkeys have their eyes open at birth and can cling to their mother's fur.

Baby-sitting
Langur mothers let other females hold and look after their babies. This makes their lives easier.

Mother's milk

Like other mammals, vervet monkey mothers make milk in their bodies to feed to their babies. They have to eat a lot of food to give them enough energy to make this milk.

Watch with mother

Monkey babies, like this spider monkey, cling to their mothers. They watch the other monkeys in the troop to learn how to climb and leap, which food is good to eat, and how to behave.

Apes and monkeys in danger

All the apes (except humans) and many monkeys are in danger of becoming extinct. The main problem is humans.

Ape crisis

Nearly all the apes, including the white-handed gibbon, will be extinct in just 20 years. People must do more to save them from hunting and habitat destruction.

Disappearing act

Marmosets, like this tufted-ear marmoset, have lost their forest homes. They are also caught and sold as pets.

Monkey madness

The rare Chinese golden monkey is threatened by hunting for its meat and fur. The trees in its forest home are also being cut down.

extinct – none left alive anywhere on earth

Saving apes and monkeys

We can help to save apes and monkeys by protecting their habitat, breeding rare ones in zoos, and finding ways for people and wild animals to live together.

Special survivor

Golden lion tamarins have been saved by protecting their forest homes in Brazil.

Finding out more

We need to find out more about apes and monkeys so we can help them survive. Scientists, like Dr Jane Goodall (right), study chimps and work to save them and their habitats.

orphan – having no mother or father

Orphan apes

If a mother ape dies or is killed, her baby needs a lot of love and care. People sometimes look after these orphans, and may one day release them back into the wild.

Monkey mobile

Make a monkey chain

Follow steps 1 to 5 to make one monkey. Then make more monkeys and hook their arms together in a long chain.

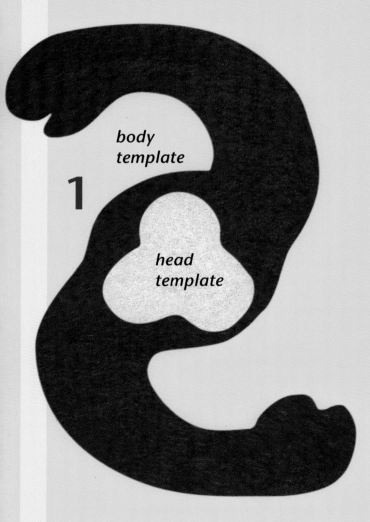

body template

1

head template

Trace the two templates in pencil and transfer the outline shapes on to a paper plate.

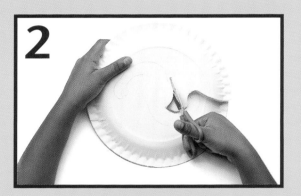

2

Using the scissors, carefully cut out the card templates. Hold the edge of the plate with one hand to stop it moving.

3

Fold a piece of brown felt in half and secure it with a pin. Trace around the body template with marker pen, then cut out.

You will need

- Tracing paper
- Pencil and black marker pen
- Paper plates
- Scissors
- Brown and cream felt
- Safety pin
- Glue

4

Glue the felt body shapes to the back and front of the card shapes. Make the faces from cream felt and glue them on.

5

Cut out four small 'D' shapes and glue them on as ears. Use a black marker pen to draw on the eyes, nose and mouth.

Eat like a chimpanzee

Make your own termite tower.
Then put food inside and use
a straw to get the food out.
It is not as easy as it looks!

You will need

- Cardboard tubes
- Sticky tape
- Scissors
- Paper plate
- Pencil
- Newspaper
- Glue or flour
- Water
- Kitchen paper
- Poster paints
- Paintbrush
- Sweets
- Drinking straws

Find four clean cardboard tubes
and tape them together with
sticky tape. Ask a parent or
friend to hold the tubes still.

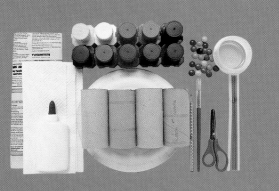

Turn a paper plate upside-down.
Hold the four tubes over the
plate and draw around them
with a pencil.

Using the scissors, carefully cut
out the holes in the paper plate.
Then tape the tubes firmly in
place over the holes.

Screw up pieces of newspaper and stick them into the gaps between the tubes. This should make a mound shape.

Mix flour and water together or use glue to paste strips of kitchen paper and newspaper over the mound. Paint it to look like mud.

Choose some sweets that are larger than the end of a straw and place them in the tubes. Suck through a straw to pull up the sweets. How many can you catch?

Monkey masks

Make a monkey face

Monkeys and apes have round heads which are perfect for making masks. Find your favourite monkey or ape in the book and make a mask of its face.

You will need
- Felt tip pen
- Tracing paper
- Coloured felt
- Scissors
- Glue
- Paper plate
- Elastic

Draw the head of the monkey on to tracing paper. Place this on to brown felt and carefully cut out around the outside edges.

Trace the face shape of the monkey on to tracing paper. Put this over the cream felt and cut it out.